D. DOUG GIBSON

GOOD
— AS —
NEW

A CHILD'S GUIDE TO
BECOMING A CHRISTIAN

LEADER'S GUIDE

college
press
Joplin, Missouri

college
press

Good as New: A Child's Guide to Becoming a Christian (Leader's Guide)
Copyright © 2000 College Press Publishing

Updated cover and text design in 2024.

All rights reserved.

ISBN: 9780899008073 (paperback)
ISBN: 9780899008257 (ePub)

Art Direction: Chad Harrington (YouPublish.com)
Cover Design: Nate Farro (YouPublish.com)

CONTENTS

INTRODUCTION

I grew up in a preacher's family. Every year my father would teach a four- week series to our 3rd–6th grade Sunday School classes on "How to Become a Christian." And every year several of our children would make a personal decision for Christ. I grew up thinking all churches did this. It wasn't until I went into the youth ministry and started serving at other churches that I learned that this is the exception, not the rule in our churches today.

One church in particular brought this point home to me. As I was interviewing for the position, one of their greatest concerns was for the new youth minister to challenge teens about becoming Christians. I took this to mean the church was very evangelistic and bringing in lots of "unchurched" teens. When I went there to serve, I discovered that it was their own children who were not making personal decisions for Christ. They were growing up in the church, faithfully attending all the right events. But many of them had reached late high school or even college without ever committing themselves to Christ. In college they were walking away from Christianity. They had no personal commitment.

Somewhere down the line the church had counted on the church camp to challenge their children, the parents had counted on the church, and the church camp had counted on the parents. There could be a lot of reasons for this, but one of the most likely was that no one wanted to "force" Christianity on their children. They didn't want to indoctrinate anyone, and in the process, they didn't encourage anyone either.

Surveys have consistently shown us that over 80% of the people who decide to accept Jesus as Lord do so before the age of 21. The longer a person waits to accept Christ, the harder it is to change established patterns of who is Lord of their life.

It is difficult to convince high schoolers that they need to let Jesus be Lord of their lives. After all, they were just then starting to have the freedom to do what they wanted. Some of them never did make that decision.

We started teaching this lesson series to our children, and they have whole-heartedly given themselves to Christ. Many of them were just waiting for someone to ask them if they wanted to be a Christian and then to show them how to make the commitment. There is a lot to be said for having the heart of a child.

This lesson series is not an indoctrination. It is an opportunity for our children to learn about our Savior and to learn what they must do to receive the salvation that comes from God.

I hope and pray this series will be as much a blessing to you as it was to me when I was growing up and continues to be in the churches where I serve.

Doug Gibson

PUBLICITY

"HOW TO BECOME A CHRISTIAN" CLASS

Beginning Sunday, March 6th, we will be starting our annual class series on becoming a Christian for all of our 3rd–6th graders. Each year we take the four Sunday school classes before Easter to teach our children about what is involved in becoming a Christian and what is then expected of them once they make that decision. For our young people who have already made their decision for Christ, this is a good review. For those who have not yet accepted Him as Lord and Savior, this is the time to ask specific questions and learn about what is involved. We'd like to encourage you to be sure to have your children here for these classes.

SAMPLE LETTER TO PARENTS

Dear Parents of 3rd–6th graders,

For some time now you have been faithfully bringing your children to church, to Sunday School, youth groups, Vacation Bible School and a variety of other church activities. You have been bringing them with you and giving them a chance to learn about our Savior and to worship Him. I commend you! You could not be doing anything more important for your children.

As children get into grade school and early junior high, they start to question everything (as if you didn't already know that!). They ask ten million "Why?" "How come?" and "Can I?" questions. They even start to question Christianity and the church. There's nothing wrong with this — it's perfectly normal (even if it does drive you up the wall). It's how they learn and gather information to start to understand the world around them and to make choices for themselves.

That's why we're having a "How to Become a Christian Class" for your children. Up until now, you have been doing the believing for your children. Christianity is your religion but not yet theirs. Sometime during the grade-school years your children start to understand this. They want to give their life to Christ but sometimes do not have the information they need to decide, and often they aren't even sure what questions to ask. At the same time, you want them to decide but are concerned: "Are they old enough?" "If I bring it up, am I pushing them into it?"

This class is designed to help us with some of these dilemmas by answering many of the questions they have about Christianity.

- The first week we talk about who Jesus is, what sin is, why it separates us from God, and why we need a Savior.
- The second week we discuss God's divine plan, and how Jesus fits into it as our Savior.
- The third week we cover the basic steps that we go through in becoming Christians.
- The fourth week we talk about what it means to live the Christian life and what God wants us to do once we accept His Son as our Savior.

At the end of the fourth week, we hand out cards that the children can sign if they want to become Christians. One of the teachers of the class will then visit with you, their parents, in the home of each of those interested to cover any questions that you or your child might have.

Our desire for this class is to: 1) give them the knowledge necessary to make a personal decision for Christ; 2) give them an opportunity to think about this decision, discuss it at home, and make a commitment that will last; and 3) help put your mind at ease that they did know what decision they were making and why.

We are going to have this class during the first Sunday School hour from March 19th to April 9th. All of our 3rd–6th graders will be in the class. If your child has already accepted Christ, it is a good review for him/her; if a decision has not yet been made, it is a good chance to learn about Him. This is a very important class for your children, so please try to have them here for it. You are welcome to sit in as well.

In His Name,

LESSON ONE:
"WHO IS JESUS?" AND "WHAT IS SIN?"

MATERIALS NEEDED FOR LESSON #1

Opening Activity: paper, pencil, opaque container

Teaching time:

- Option #1: "Who Is This Jesus Anyway" crossword puzzle and Match-up worksheet in workbook, pencils
- Option #2: Active Learning Activity: old newspapers, tape, several large trash bags
- A children's workbook for each child for the "Who Is This Jesus Anyway?" crossword puzzle and the "Match-up" activities

OBJECTIVES FOR LESSON #1

If our children are going to understand what God has offered to us through His Son and recognize that they need this gift, we need to start by answering three basic questions: What is a Christian? Who is Jesus? What is sin?

OPENING ACTIVITY

5-7 minutes of activity with a 2-3 minute lead into lesson

Charades

Preparation: Print 10-20 different people or animals on small pieces of paper. For example: a cowboy, a cheerleader, a ballerina, a football player, a monkey, a dog, a cat. Pick occupations or animals that will be relatively easy to pantomime and will not unnecessarily embarrass the student. Place the small pieces of paper in an opaque container.

Activity: Ask for a volunteer from the class to come up and pantomime (act out without using their voice) the person or animal they draw from the container. Allow the kids to freely guess what they think the student is acting out. The first person to guess the correct answer will be either the next student to do a charade, or if they have already done a charade, they may choose another student to go next. Move quickly from charade to charade to keep the interest level up.

Discussion: After completing the game, ask the class these questions.

- **If you had picked a piece of paper that said a "Christian" on it, how would you have acted that out?** You should get a variety of answers such as praying, reading a Bible, going to church, doing a good deed, etc. Be sure to praise them for their answers.
- Most of the things we mentioned are things that Christians do. If I ask you: **"What is a Christian?" what would you say?** Again, you will get a variety of answers. Use these answers to get the most basic definition:

A Christian is someone who believes and follows the teachings of Christ. To put it even more simply, it is to be Christlike.

THE LESSON
PART ONE: "WHO IS JESUS?"

If we want to be a football player, an actor, or a musician, we will imitate those people. We try to be like them, dress like them, talk like them and act like them. If we are to be like Christ, then it will be helpful for us to find out who He is and some of what He does.

Discussion

- Ask the class: Where do we look to find out about Jesus?
- Ask the class: Who is Jesus? What does the Bible tell us about Jesus? Encourage them to give a variety of answers. Some answers might be: "Son of God," "Messiah," "Teacher," "Savior," etc. The "Who Is This Jesus Any- way?" solution sheet at the end of this lesson will give you some verses that you might use at this time to get more answers from your students.

WORKBOOK ACTIVITY

The "Who Is This Jesus Anyway?" puzzle in our workbooks can give us some more answers about what the Bible tells us about Jesus. The "Match-up" worksheet can help your students better understand some of the titles that Jesus is called. (You can have the students do these activities now, or you can send them home to be done with their parents. If you're planning on doing the Active Learning activity later in the lesson, then you probably won't have time to do this puzzle in the normal Sunday School hour).

- Ask the class: What kinds of things did Jesus do while He was alive here on earth? What kinds of feelings (emotions) does the Bible tell us Jesus had while He was here? Again, encourage a variety of answers. A few specific verses from our workbook include:

Mark 1:13 ....He was tempted	Luke 4:15........................He taught people
Luke 5:16................................He prayed	Luke 7:21..................... He healed the sick
Matt. 8:24-26............................He slept	Mark 10:21....................... He loved people
Matt. 14:14.............. He had compassion	John 11:35................................ Jesus wept
Luke 7:12–15........... He raised the dead	Matt. 28:5–6........ He rose from the dead
Luke 2:52............ Jesus grew in wisdom and stature and in favor with God and men.	

Obviously, we can use a lot of different words to describe who Jesus is and what He did. But most of our descriptions fall naturally into three categories:

- **The first category is the divine (or Godlike) nature of Jesus. Which of our answers fit in this category?**
- **The second one involves Jesus' life here on earth. Which of our answers fit in here?** His life here on earth was very similar to the ones that we live. Isn't it nice to know that Jesus understands us?
- **The third category is the purpose for Jesus' coming to earth, living and then dying for us. Which of your answers fits into this category?** It's O.K. if the children can't think of the ones that fit this area because this is the area that we're going to explore as we learn about becoming a Christian.

PART TWO: "WHAT IS SIN?"

If you were in a burning building and a fireman came and rescued you, we would say, "He **saved** you from the fire." If you were drowning in the pool and the lifeguard pulled you out, we would say, "He **saved** you from drowning." You could call them your **saviors** because they had saved your life from dangers that were going to destroy it.

If we are going to call Jesus our **Savior**, then we need to know what He's saving us from and why we need to be saved in the first place.

Discussion

- What is it that Jesus is saving us from? If the class answers this question with "Hell," ask them what it is that we do that would send us to Hell.
- What are some sins that people commit? Exodus 20:1-17 and Galatians 5:19-21 give a couple of lists of a few of the possible sins.
- How do we know what is a sin and what is not? Some answers might be "the Bible tells us," "Mom and Dad tell me," or "God tells us in the Bible."
- So, if God tells us what to do (or not to do), and we do the opposite, then that is sin, right? Right.
- This gives us our basic definition for sin. Sin is simply disobeying God, even if it's lying, killing, cheating, or disobeying our parents. If we do something other than what God has told us to do, we are being disobedient to Him and that is sin.
- Obviously we've all blown it. In fact Romans 3:23 tells us: "All people have sinned and are not good enough for God's glory." You may have lived a pretty good life, but if you've blown it even once (and we all have), then you are a sinner and in need of a Savior.

Now we've got an activity that is going to help us to better understand what sin does, and how Jesus saves us from it.

SIN-SENSATION

Active Learning Illustration: allow 20 minutes for this activity, with at least 5 minutes for the discussion at the end.

Preparation: You will need several old newspapers (at least 10 standard newspaper pages per student) several rolls of scotch or masking tape, and several large trash bags.

Activity

1. Divide your class into groups of 3-8 students each. The number of groups you have will be determined by the size of classroom that you have. If your classroom is relatively small, keep the number of groups small, with each group having more students. If your classroom is spacious, then have several smaller groups of students.

2. Each group must have a sufficient supply of newspapers and at least one roll of tape.

3. Once your class has been divided, tell the class that they will have 10 minutes to build a hiding place for their group. It must be large enough for all of them to fit inside of it. After the 10 minutes you will judge each group by seeing which team has the least amount of their bodies visible through the newspapers. They may use only the tape, newspapers and themselves. They cannot tape to the walls, floor, chairs, tables, etc. (your janitors will still love you this way).

4. It may be necessary for you to "fudge" a little on the time, give them more if they need it, or less if you're running out of class time. Give them a "one minute"

warning, and a 20-second countdown so that they will know when they need to pile into their hiding place.

IT'S IMPORTANT THAT THEY *ALL* GET IN THEIR HIDING PLACES AND STAY IN THEM UNTIL YOU TELL THEM TO COME OUT

5. Once the "judging" has begun, they need to be quiet so that they can hear you.

6. Take your time "judging" the different groups. You're about to start the next teaching time. The more uncomfortable, cramped, and hot they get (within reason) the better.

TEACHING APPLICATION: (Do this while they are still in their paper hiding places.)

1. Tell each group: **Think of two sins that people commit.**

2. Ask each group: **What two sins have you chosen?**

3. Tell them that you are going to start moving around the room. You will tap each hiding place, and when you do, they are to start saying their "sins" out loud, starting soft and then getting louder and louder. They are to keep "sinning" until you come and tap their hiding places again. At that time, they will get softer and softer until they stop saying their "sins" altogether. Remind everyone in order for this to work, they shouldn't be talking at the times they're supposed to be quiet.

4. Start saying the word "forgiveness" in a regular voice. Keep saying "forgiveness" as you go around and tap each group. Let them be loud for a while and then go around and tap each group

again until they get quiet. All the while you'll be saying the word "forgiveness" over and over.

5. When all is quiet again, tell them to stay in their hiding places a little longer (they should be groaning, and complaining by now).

- Ask them: **Could you hear me saying "forgiveness" all of the time?**
- Ask them: **Why couldn't you hear the forgiveness that I was offering you?** You'll get a variety of answers along the line of "we were sinning too loud."
- Ask them: **How did it feel to be trapped in your hiding places?** You may get answers like: "hot," "cramped," "his foot is in my face," etc.

6. Tell them to stay in their hiding places, until you come over and tap their group and say the word "forgiveness." At that time, they can break free. (If any group breaks free early, have them get back down on the floor and let the other groups bury them in their old newspaper, and then tap that group and say "forgiveness" and they can break out.)

7. This will immediately cause a newspaper wad fight. Let them go at it for a minute (get involved in it yourself) and then have the group put the trash in the trash bags provided.

Closing (5 minutes)
Have everyone sit down again for your closing discussion.

Discussion
- How did it feel to be building the group hiding places? ("It was fun," "Ours was the best," "I like to belong," etc.)

- How can sin be like this? "It seems like it will be fun at first," "Everybody else is doing it," or "I liked belonging to a little group."
- After you had been under the newspapers for a while was it fun any- more? Why not? "It got uncomfortable," "I got a cramp," or "I couldn't breathe."
- That's exactly what sin does to us. It promises to be fun or exciting, but it winds up being confining, and uncomfortable — not at all what you had expected. In fact, sin separates us from God and traps us.
- How did it feel to be set free? "It was great," "I was so hot and now I'm cool again," "It was so cramped and uncomfortable and now I can stretch."
- That's what Jesus has done by being our Savior. He forgives us of our sins, and sets us free from sin. This is what it feels like to be a Christian.

Next week we're going to be learning about how this happens. We're going to discuss God's plan and just how Jesus fits into it as our Savior.

ANSWER TO WORKBOOK ACTIVITIES

WHO IS THIS JESUS ANYWAY?

Look up the following verses and fill in the blanks. Find the words that describe Jesus and fit into the crossword puzzle.

DOWN:

1. John 6:35 "Then Jesus declared, 'I am the bread of **LIFE**. He who comes to me will never go hungry, and he who believes in me will never be thirsty.'"

2. Matt 1:23 "The virgin will be with child and give birth to a son, and they will call him **EMMANUEL** — which means 'God with us.'"

3. Matt 3:17 "And a voice from heaven said 'This is my **SON** , whom I love; with him I am well pleased.

6. Luke 4:18 "The Spirit of the Lord is on me, because he has **ANOINTED** me to preach the good news to the poor" (this fulfills an Old Testament Prophecy."

8. Colossians 1:16 "For by him all things were **CREATED**: things in heaven and on earth . . . ."

9. John 13:13 "You call me **TEACHER** and 'Lord', and rightly so, for that is what I am."

ACROSS

4. Revelation 19:16 "On his robe and on his thigh he has this name written: **KING OF KING AND LORD OF LORDS**."

5. John 4:42 "They said to the woman: 'We no longer believe just because of what you said; now we have heard for ourselves, and we know that this man is really the **SAVIOR** of the world.'"

7. John 4:25-26 "The woman said, 'I know that the **MESSIAH**' (called Christ) 'is coming. When he comes, he will explain everything to us'. Then Jesus declared, 'I who speak to you am he.'"

10. Ephesians 2:20 "You are . . . members of God's household, built on the foundation of the apostles and prophets, with Christ Jesus as the chief **CORNERSTONE**.

11. John 14:6 "I am the **WAY** and the truth and the life. No one comes to the father except through me."

12. I am the **VINE**; you are the branches. If a man remains in me and in him, he will bear much fruit. Apart from me you can do nothing."

13. John 1:14 "The **WORD** became flesh and made his dwelling among us. We have seen his glory, the glory of the One and Only, who came from the father."

(this will be filled in completely)

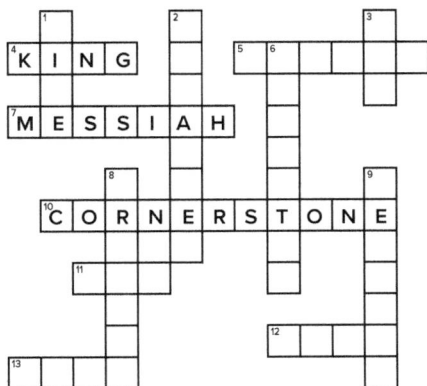

ANSWER TO WORKBOOK ACTIVITIES

MATCH-UP

Congratulations! You've just discovered some of the words used to describe Jesus. Do you know what they mean? In this activity match the words describing Jesus with their meanings by drawing a line to connect them.

Son of God	Someone who rescues us from danger or from dying.
Anointed One	Means "God with us."
Bread of Life	The only path that allows us to come before God is through Jesus.
Son of David	Jesus is the "top dog"; He sits at the right hand of God and is greater than all others no matter what their "title."
Emmanuel	Jesus' Father is God.
Messiah	Jesus gives us everything that we need. Without Him we would die, but through Him we produce fruit in our lives.
Cornerstone	Another word for Christ or Savior. This is a word the Jews would use when they were looking for the Promised One from God.
The Vine	Another term for Christ. Jesus was specifically chosen and dedicated for a job. He was set apart from the beginning of time by God to die for us. This term has a picture of pouring oil over some- one to dedicate them for a certain job.
The Way	Jesus was a descendant of David. He was the chosen descendant who had been promised to come and be a blessing to all the nations of the world.
Savior	Jesus gives us everything that we need to live; without Him we would die.
King of Kings	Jesus is the basis upon which we build our lives. This term refers to the most important part of a building. The building would fall apart without it.

LESSON TWO:
TRUTH OR CONSEQUENCES

MATERIALS NEEDED FOR LESSON #2

Opening activity: Empty 1-gallon jug, a piece of rope, and a large piece of hard rock candy, or something else solid about the size of a baseball.

Teaching time:

- Option #1: Tape recorder with blank tape
- Closing activity: blindfold, basket, 3 small tennis balls (or other light balls)
- A student workbook for each child for the "Missing the Mark," "Pictures of Hell," and "Rhyming Tombstones" activities.

OBJECTIVES FOR LESSON #2

Lesson #2 will focus on helping our children understand the consequences of sin, God's plan for our salvation, and how Jesus fits into this plan as our Savior.

OPENING ACTIVITY: (6-8 MINUTES)

Preparation: You will need to take an empty one-gallon jug and cut a hole in the side of it. This hole needs to be just barely large enough for the rock candy or baseball-sized object that you choose to fit into it (in other words, you don't want the hole to be so large that the object will easily fall out, if the kids shake the jug or tilt it). Tie a rope to the handle of the jug and tie it to something in your classroom.

Activity: Show the milk jug to your kids. Then show them the rock candy and tell them that you are going to put the candy in the jug and would like for a volunteer to put her hand in the opening and take it out. (The plastic milk jug is obviously of limited strength, so start with some smaller, less aggressive students; eventually one of the older children will pull hard enough to tear the plastic and get the candy out.) Give several children an opportunity to take the candy out. After several have attempted it or after someone finally succeeds, read "The Monkey Trap" to them.

THE MONKEY TRAP

In Africa the tribesmen have a very simple way of trapping monkeys. They hollow out a coconut and cut a small hole just big enough for a monkey's hand to fit into the coconut. The tribesmen will go into the area of trees where the monkeys live and tie the coconut to a stake. They will take a shiny object or a piece of candy and hold it up for the monkeys to see, and then they will slowly place the object into the coconut. After the tribesmen leave, a monkey will come down out of the trees, stick its hand into the coconut and grab the candy. The only problem is that when it makes a fist inside the coconut, it can't pull its hand back out. The monkey wants the object so much that it won't let go. The tribesmen simply go back to the trap and put it in a cage. Some monkeys have been known to starve to death rather than let go of the bait.

Explain to them that we were (or might be) strong enough to tear the plastic, but there is no way for the monkey to tear the coconut.

Discussion: After reading the story, ask the class these questions.

- **If he can't tear his way out, how could the monkey escape?** You should get the obvious answer, "He could just let go."
- **Why won't he simply let go?** They may say because he's "stupid." Keep them going until you get the "because he wants what is in the trap" kind of answers.
- **How is this like sin?** "We want it so bad that we won't let go of it, even when we know that it's hurting us."
- **How does the monkey trap remind you about what we talked about last week?** If they need prompting, remind them about the paper forts they built and how they were "trapped" in sin.
- **What was the definition for sin that we learned last week?** Sin is being disobedient to God.

THE LESSON
PART ONE: "THE CONSEQUENCES OF SIN"
(10 MINUTES)

Ask the class the following questions. If they don't know the answers or are unfamiliar with the story of the Fall of Man, have them look up and read Genesis 3, or you could paraphrase Genesis 3 for them.

- **What was the first sin?** Adam and Eve eating the forbidden fruit
- **Where did it happen?** In the Garden
- **How were Adam and Eve punished?** Eve was to have pain in childbirth. She would desire her husband, and he would rule over her. Adam would have to work the ground for food, and it would be difficult work. Adam and Eve were

both kicked out of the garden. They would both grow old and die. These answers are found in Genesis 3:16-24

Sin had direct consequences for Adam and Eve. It also has a direct impact on our lives today. Ask your class: **What are some of the consequences that we face for the sins that we commit?** (For example: disobedience to parents may result in grounding, or spreading lies about someone may cost us some- one's friendship or people may no longer trust us.)

But those are not the only consequences of sin. The greatest consequence of sin is the one that we will face at the end of our lives. Hebrews 9:27 tells us: "Everyone must die once. After a person dies, he is judged."

Ask the class: **What is going to happen on the Day of Judgment when we all stand before God?**

The greatest consequence of Adam and Eve's sin is that they were no longer able to walk in the garden with God. They had separated themselves from God because of their disobedience. When we stand before God on the judgment day, our sins will separate us from God as well.

What do we call the place that God will send those who are separated from Him?

Hell.

What does the Bible tell us Hell will be like?

WORKBOOK ACTIVITY If you have the time and want to go into more detail on the descriptions of Hell, at this time have the children do the "Picture of Hell" activity in the workbook.

Notice that each description of Hell is of a very uncomfortable place where there is no one to care for the needs of those who are there. That is because the worst thing about Hell is that it is a place where God is not. He cannot care for our needs there.

GOD'S PLAN STEP ONE: (8 MINUTES)

Now all of this started with Adam and Eve eating from the tree in the Garden. **How many rules did Adam and Eve have in the garden?** (just one)

> **If God had not put the tree in the Garden, could Adam and Eve have sinned?** No they could not have sinned. Sin is disobedience and there would have been no opportunity to disobey.

> **Do you think that God knew that if He put the tree there, Adam and Eve were going to eat from it?** Of course He did.

> **If God knew they would eat from the tree, then why did He put the tree in the Garden?** He could have forced us to obey Him, but He wanted people who would choose to obey Him.

ACTIVE LEARNING OPTION: (3-4 MINUTES)

Preparation: Bring a phone with you to class.

Activity: Go to the recording app on the phone, hit "record," and then spend a minute or two recording outrageous compliments about yourself. Be sure to include all areas of your being, your good looks, great personality, charm, intelligence, etc. After this has gone on for a while, stop recording and play back how wonderful you think you are. As you listen to your compliments, respond to them as if someone was really complimenting you. Say things like: "That's so kind of you"; "Oh, you're just saying that." Be sure to "gush" over the comments.

Debrief: The students will be smiling or laughing by now. Stop the recording and ask them: What's the problem? Don't all of these compliments mean anything? Why not?

> That's exactly why God put the tree in the Garden. He could have made robots who would have no choice but to say nice things about Him all day long, but He wanted people who would freely choose to follow and love Him.

> If you tell your parents you love them without being forced to, it means something. This is what God wanted, so He gave us a choice. We could choose to love and obey Him, or we could choose not to.

GOD'S PLAN STEP TWO: (8 MINUTES)

God told Adam and Eve that if they ate from the tree they would surely die. Why did He not kill them when they first ate from the tree? **Why doesn't He kill us the first time that we disobey our parents (for example, the first time we don't clean up our room, or take out the trash when we're told to)?**

> Romans 3:25 tells us "God gave Jesus as a way to forgive sin through faith. And all of this is because of the blood of Jesus' death. This showed that God always does what is right and fair. God was right in the past when He was patient and did not punish people for their sins."

God put off punishing us with death when we first sin, because out of His love for us He wants us to come back to Him.

When it's time to do something, you can do it one of two ways: 1) You can do it yourself, or 2) you can ask for help. Most of us like to do things for ourselves. We can't wait to be able to dress ourselves, pick out our own clothes, go to a friend's house by riding our skates or our bike. As you get older, this will be even more true. You'll want to drive your own car, have your own place to live, come in at night when you want to. **Have you ever been in the car with someone who has gotten lost, but won't stop to ask for help?**

The Old Testament part of our Bible teaches us about both trying to do it yourself and asking for help.

As you read through the Old Testament, you will find that God has more rules for His people. The 10 commandments are some of them; there are several dozen others as well. Basically, He told His people that if they wanted to try to be good enough to please Him, they had to obey all of these rules. Well, if Adam and Eve couldn't obey one rule in the garden, how was anyone else supposed to obey all the rules found in the Old Testament? The answer is simple: they couldn't. They needed to (and we do too) learn that you can't get to Heaven on your own. You can't be good enough; you can't impress God with your good looks; nothing you do can earn your right to go to Heaven.

WORKBOOK ACTIVITY Your class can do the "Tombstones" exercise in their workbook at this time if you wish. This activity reminds our class that they can't do anything to get to Heaven on their own.

The people in the Old Testament quickly realized this, and they started crying out for a savior, someone who could take away their sins.

While they were waiting for the Savior to come, God taught them a lesson through the sacrifice of animals. He instructed His people to go and take the finest animals from their flocks and kill them and burn them on an altar in His temple as a covering for their sins. **Could the blood of an animal take away their sins? (No) Then why do you think God asked them to do this?**

1. They needed to know that the consequence of sin is death.
2. He was teaching them that only a pure and blameless (sinless) sacrifice could cover their sins.
3. He was teaching them about the Savior who was coming who would have to die for their sins.

Overall, the Old Testament clearly shows us that we can't make it to Heaven on our own. We need a Savior!!!

GOD'S PLAN: PART THREE (8 MINUTES)

God could have killed all of us the first time we sinned, but because He loves us He has put off punishment, so we can have an opportunity to be saved.

God knew in the beginning we would sin and we would be unable to make it to Heaven on our own, so He chose to send His Son Jesus to be our Savior.

Can anyone tell us what John 3:16 says? (If not, let's look it up.)

Three things are obvious:

1. Jesus came and lived a sinless life. He deserved to go to Heaven because He obeyed all that God has asked of us.
2. We have sinned. We deserve to be punished.
3. God is fair. In all fairness those who have sinned should be punished; those who don't sin shouldn't be punished.

But God also loves us, so in His love He has said He will let someone else be punished in our place. But that person who is being punished in our place cannot be deserving of punishment himself.

Think about school. If you and your friend each get a detention for talking and you show up for the detention and say, "I'm serving both of our detentions at the same time," is that going to work? Of course not. You have to serve your own detention.

CIVIL WAR ILLUSTRATION

In the American Civil War the North had all men of a certain age sign up for the draft. If your name was chosen, you were required to go fight in the war. But in reality the North didn't care who showed up just as long as the right number of soldiers were mustered for battle. If 10,000 men were drafted, then 10,000 men had to show up. Many of the men who were drafted had families that they needed to take care of, so the North would allow someone else to take that person's place. But that person replacing the drafted person couldn't have already been drafted himself. If he had been drafted, he had to show up in his own place. But if he had not been drafted, then he could go to war in someone else's place.

God has allowed the same thing to happen with us. If someone who has lived a sinless life freely offers to take my punishment on my behalf, God will allow that to happen. God is fair, and in all fairness, disobedience has to be punished; but He is also loving, so in love He will allow another to pay the price. We call that person our Savior, and His name is Jesus Christ. He is the Son of

God. No one but the Son of God could live a sinless life and be able to take our punishment.

Hebrews 9:27 told us about how we would all be judged after death. But the verses around it give us hope. Hebrews 9:26-28 says: "Christ came only once and for all time. He came at just the right time to take away all sin by sacrificing himself. Everyone must die once. After a person dies, he is judged. So, Christ was offered as a sacrifice one time to take away the sins of many people. And he will come a second time, but not to offer himself for sin. He will come again to bring salvation to those who are waiting for him."

CLOSING ACTIVITY: MISSING THE MARK (5 MINUTES)

Preparation: You will need a basket or trash can and 3 tennis or other light weight balls.

Activity: Blindfold a volunteer from the class. Set up a basket (trash can) as a target on the other side of the room. Spin your volunteer around 8-9 times to disorient her, and then give her three shots to try to hit the basket (don't aim her towards the goal after spinning her). Don't let the rest of the class help.

Did she hit the target? Why not? You'll get answers like, "She couldn't see the basket," or "You had her facing the wrong direction."

Now take the blindfold off and let her try again.

Did she make all of her baskets this time? Did she make any baskets? Why didn't she make all of them? You should get answers like "No one can make every basket all of the time," or "She's not a good enough shot."

Now let her try one more time, but this time have 3-4 other volunteers from the class stand around the goal. Their job is to make sure that the balls go in the basket. Let your volunteer shoot again.

Did she make the baskets? How was she able to do it? You'll get answers along the line of "She had help."

Another way the Bible looks at sin is to describe it in a word picture. The picture is that of a person using a bow to shoot arrows at a target. When he hits the bullseye, he's hitting his target. When he misses, he's missing the mark (or target), and that's another picture of sin. When we miss what God wants us to be aiming for, we are sinning.

Our game and this word picture of an archer missing his mark help us to understand the reason for the Old Testament. If we didn't know what sin was or what God wanted us to do, we would be like the blindfolded shooter. There's no way that we could obey God, because we wouldn't know what we were aiming for. Even when we know what God wants us to do, we can't hit the target all of the time, so God has provided a Savior to help us hit our target, to correct us when we miss, and most of all to allow us to be forgiven of our mistakes.

WORKBOOK ACTIVITY The workbook activity "Missing the Mark" involves another version of the above activity that can be done in the workbooks. Next week we're going to talk about what we must do to be forgiven by God and restored into his family.

ANSWER TO WORKBOOK ACTIVITIES:

TOMBSTONES: best, money, car, looks, friends, head

LESSON THREE:
THE NUTS AND BOLTS OF BECOMING A CHRISTIAN

MATERIALS NEEDED FOR LESSON #3

Opening activity: tape player with tape

Teaching time:

- Option #1: bag of raw spaghetti (30 sticks per person), bag of small marshmallows (20 per person)
- Option #2: flash paper, metal pan, matches
- Option #3: a cross, extra paper, thumbtacks
- A student workbook for each child for "The Cross Is the Bridge," "Steps in Becoming a Christian" Scripture Search, and "Matching the Definitions" activities

OBJECTIVES FOR LESSON #3

The students will come to appreciate that God has already done all the work for us. Becoming a Christian is an easy process because God wanted to be sure that no one thinks he has done it on his own.

OPENING ACTIVITY: (10 MINUTES)

Preparation: Bring your phone or computer with you to class so you can play music through it. Arrange the chairs in a circle. Have enough chairs for each student, then remove one chair.

Play a quick game of musical chairs, eliminating the chairs (and students) one at a time until you have a winner. Take special note of how the students behave and how they put their needs above the others.

Play the game again, but this time as you eliminate the chairs, don't eliminate the students. Instead have them sit on each other's laps as the chairs disappear. Continue playing until there is only one chair with all of the students "sitting" in it.

Notice the difference of attitudes in the students and how they play the game.

Arrange your chairs as you normally would, and then discuss the two games that you just played.

Ask your class the following questions: **In the first round how did it feel to be eliminated? How did the person who won act? Did he play fair? Did he play too rough?**

Now contrast that to the second game. **How did it feel in the second game? Were there any losers? Who was the winner? Which game was more fun?**

Over the last two weeks, we've discovered several ways to lose the prize of going to Heaven, and we've discussed one way to win the prize of going to Heaven. **How can we lose the prize?** (by sinning or trying to save ourselves) **How can we win the prize?** (through Christ Jesus) Today we're going to talk about the basic steps in becoming a Christian.

LESSON:
PART ONE: WHAT HAS GOD DONE? (10 MINUTES)
As we talk about what we need to do to become a Christian, it is important for us to be reminded that we can't do anything to earn it. You can't be good enough. Remember, everyone has sinned and fallen short of the goal. You can't do anything to wash away the sin in your life.

God has chosen to do the hard part for us. He has done this out of love.

First of all, He has chosen to let someone else be punished in our place. He didn't have to do that, but because He loves us, He has allowed it.

Secondly, God sent His Son to pay the price for our sins.

We all know that Jesus died on the cross. Let's take a minute or two to look at the price our Savior paid for the forgiveness of our sins.

THE PRICE CHRIST PAID:

The crucifixion was one of the cruelest and most painful ways for a person to die. The Romans used it to discourage others from doing what those crucified had done. In the Gospels we read that this is what happened to Jesus as He paid the price for our sins.

1. The soldiers seized Him in the garden, and all of His friends deserted Him. Have you ever had friends let you down when you needed them? This was the start of Jesus' paying our price.

2. He stood trial before the Sanhedrin. People lied about Him. They spit in His face, beat Him and struck Him with their fists. Others blindfolded Him and slapped Him, saying, "Prophesy for us, Christ. Who hit you?" Then they bound Him and took Him to Pilate.

3. He stood trial before Pilate. Pilate offered to have Jesus or Barabbas (a convicted murderer) set free. The crowd chose Barabbas. Then Pilate had Jesus flogged and crucified. A flogging in Roman times usually involved being hit (usually 39 times) with a short whip that had several strips of leather joined together at

the handle. Often these strips of leather would have glass, nails or sharp rocks tied to the ends to inflict even more pain. They were used on the back and on the chest of the victim.

4. Pilate's soldiers gathered around Jesus and stripped Him and put a scarlet robe on Him. They put a crown of thorns (more like 2-inch spikes) on His head. They mocked Him, spit in His face, and beat Him over the head with a staff (a long piece of wood). This would have, of course, driven the thorns even farther into Jesus' head. Then, they put His own clothes back on Him and took Him out to be crucified.

5. A crucified person was required to carry his own cross (or cross beam) to the crucifixion site. Jesus was so weak from the beatings that He was unable to carry His own cross all of the way.

6. To crucify a person, you nailed or tied his arms to a cross. When nails were used, they were about the size of our railroad spikes. Then they would lift the cross up in the air in a very public place so that everyone could see the person. As a person was on the cross, his outspread arms made his lungs collapse; in order to breathe he had to stand up on the nails going through his feet, and then when the pain got too bad, he would sink down again. Every breath was extremely painful.

7. While Jesus was being crucified, the soldiers stripped Him and gambled for His clothes. People walking by, the guards, and even one of the thieves being crucified, all insulted and mocked Him.

This is not a very pretty image, but it is what Jesus went through for us. Let us never forget that God and His Son have done the hard work for us. We should be very thankful that we didn't have to take that punishment for our sins.

The sections of Scripture that cover what Jesus went through during His trial and crucifixion are: Matt. 26:14–27:56, Mark 14:12–15:41, Luke 22:47–23:49, and John 18:1–19:37.

PART TWO: WHAT MUST I DO? (20 MINUTES)

Active Option #1: Hearing and believing frustration: To give the students a proper perspective on the first two steps in the salvation process using this activity to frustrate them.

Preparation: Bring enough raw spaghetti for each student to have 30 sticks. You'll start with 20 and then use the rest for the second round. You'll also need a bag of small marshmallows — enough for about 20 per student.

Round #1: Give each student 20 sticks of raw spaghetti and 10 small marshmallows (if you don't have these supplies, you can use a piece of paper and a pencil). Tell your class that they will have 3 minutes to complete their project. Now tell them to get started. Don't give them any more instructions. If they ask you what to do, tell them that they have everything they need. Walk around the class during the 3 minutes randomly telling the kids, "Hey that's good," or "No, no, that's not right."

After the time is up, "judge" who did the best job. They were supposed to be trying to build the tallest object they could (or if you're using the paper, they were supposed to be drawing a tree). When the kids tell you that you're not being fair, ask them why. They'll let you know that you didn't tell them what to do.

Round #2: Say "O.K. This time I'll tell you what to do." Start over again (hand out new supplies, if necessary). This time give them several instructions. Make sure that they even contradict each other. For example, tell them: This time we're going to see who can build the tallest structure. Make sure that it is only two inches high. Use only marshmallows, but don't use the marshmallows. It has to be a perfect square, but it can only have three sides. Give enough contradicting instructions to confuse your kids, and then give them 3 minutes to build their object. Again, walk around the room and randomly tell the kids good things and bad things.

After the time is up, "judge" who did the best job. This time they were supposed to build a rectangle (or if you're using the paper, they were supposed to draw a flagpole). Ask the kids what was wrong with this activity. They'll still tell you that you didn't tell them what to do. Play innocent with them, "What do you mean? Didn't I tell you to build a rectangle" (make sure that you said this at least once during the conflicting instructions)? Of course you did, but they didn't know to believe you.

Tell them that these two activities teach us about the first two steps in becoming a Christian. Can anyone guess what they might be?

The first time you didn't know what to do because no one had told you what to do. The first step in becoming a Christian is hearing about Christ. Many people in the world today have never heard about Jesus, but you have, and that's the first step to becoming a Christian.

The second time you heard the instructions, but you didn't know which instruction to believe. That's the second step to becoming a Christian. It's not enough to just hear about Jesus, you have to believe that He really is the Son of God.

The verses that are in the workbook relating to these two steps are:

.Hearing: Romans 10:17; 10:14

Believing/Faith: John 20:21; Romans 3:22; Mark 16:16; and Acts 16:30-31

Most of you have been going to church for a while and have already taken these first two steps toward becoming a Christian.

The third step in becoming a Christian is described by the word "repent." What does repent mean?

Repent is a visual word that helps us to follow God. It comes from the days of the Roman Empire. The Roman legion would be marching down the road when the centurion would yell out the word "repent," and the legion would turn around and start marching the other way. This is just like today when the drill sergeant says, "About face!" and the soldiers in our army turn around and march the other way.

In our lives before a person becomes a Christian, he is the "general" of his life and issues the orders and does what he wants to, but when he becomes a Christian, God becomes his "General," and he marches according to His orders. We repent when we stop doing what we want to, turn around and start doing what God wants us to do. We quit disobeying Him and start to be obedient.

The verses that we have listed in the workbook relating to repentance are Acts 2:38; Luke 13:5 and 15:10.

WHAT ARE THE FIRST THREE STEPS IN BECOMING A CHRISTIAN?

Hearing, Believing and Repenting

The fourth step is confession.

Confessing is what a criminal does when he admits to the judge that he committed a crime. He confesses when he admits that he did wrong. If you are to become a Christian, you need to confess before God that you are a sinner and ask Him for forgiveness. Basically, you need to confess to God that you've blown it and that you need a Savior.

Confessing, for a Christian, has a second meaning as well. Just as you can confess that you have done something wrong, you can also confess that you've done something right. We call this the Good Confession. It's what you do when you confess to (or tell) others that you are a Christian and that you believe that Jesus is the Son of God and your Savior.

To become Christians, we must confess to God that we are sinners and ask Him to forgive us. We also need to start to confess Jesus before our friends.

The verses listed in the workbook relating to confession are Romans 10:9- 10 and 1 John 1:9

WHAT ARE THE FIRST FOUR STEPS IN BECOMING A CHRISTIAN?

Hearing, Believing, Repenting and Confessing

There is still one more step to becoming a Christian. That is baptism.

The verses listed in the workbook relating to baptism are Acts 2:28; Acts 16:33 and Matt 28:19.

The act of being baptized is actually very simple, but it holds several meanings for us.

The first is simply an act of obedience. If we have truly repented and are letting God give the orders, we have to be obedient to Him. Jesus told us to be baptized (Matt. 28:19). Baptism is when we first start showing our obedience to Him.

The second is a picture of cleansing. Titus 3:4-5 talks about this. When we are dirty, we take a bath. Now, we know that water can't wash our sins away, but baptism reminds us that we come to God dirty with all of our sins and He washes us clean through the blood of His Son. Baptism is when we are visibly reminded of our being cleansed of our sins.

The third meaning has to do with death. Romans 6:4 talks about this aspect. When someone dies, their body is buried in the ground. When we are baptized, we have an image of ourselves being buried in the water. As far as God is concerned, we leave our old sinful life dead and in the past. When we come out of the water, we are brand new without sin in God's eyes. Baptism is a picture of our sinful lives dying and of our "rebirth" into new life and God's family.

The fourth meaning is that baptism is an outward act that publicly demonstrates your decision to become a Christian. It is when you publicly proclaim to everyone that Jesus is Lord of your life.

WHAT ARE THE FIVE BASIC STEPS IN BECOMING A CHRISTIAN?

Hearing, Believing, Repenting, Confessing and Being Baptized

WORKBOOK ACTIVITY The "What Does It Mean?" activity in the workbook can be used as an additional reinforcement tool at this point. It goes over the definitions of the steps to becoming a Christian one more time. Answers to this activity are found on page 42.

CLOSING:

Option #2: (5-7 minutes)

Preparation: You will need to have enough "flash" paper for each student to have a 3" x 5" piece of paper. You will need a metal pan, pencils for each student, and matches.

*Flash paper can be purchased at any novelty or magic trick store. It will be damp when you purchase it (for safety reasons) and comes in 8" x 11" sheets. You can cut them into smaller sheets and then allow them to dry out before you use them. You might want to experiment on a couple of sheets before you do it in class, just so you're comfortable with how flash paper works.

Activity: Give each student a small (3" x 5") piece of flash paper. Have each of them write on it a list of sins that they've committed in their lives. Have them fold up the paper and place it in the metal pan. Tell the children: **I'm going to show you what happens to all of your sins when you become a Christian.** Have the kids keep back several feet from the pan. Light a match and toss it in the pile of flash paper. The flash paper will ignite and disappear in an impressive flash (don't stand too close or your eyebrows might disappear too!) When the flash is gone, so are the pieces of paper, and the sins that were on them.

Option #3: (5-7 minutes)

If you're not comfortable using the flash paper, use this activity.

Preparation: Build a cross ahead of time. Use materials that will allow you to thumbtack something to it (cardboard, wood, etc.). Bring extra paper and thumbtacks with you.

Activity: Hand out a piece of paper and have your students write out a list of sins they have committed. Tell them that no one else is going to look at the list; it is between them and God. Give them 2-3 minutes to work on their lists. Now tell your kids that when Jesus died on the cross, He died to set us free from our sins. So, when we become Christians, we leave our sins at the cross on which Jesus died. Have the kids one at a time go up to the cross and "nail" their sins to the cross. Remind them that our sins helped to put Jesus on the cross, but because of His love for us, we can leave them there. God forgives us through the sacrifice of His Son.

FINAL THOUGHT

Forgiveness of sins is only one of the many things that God has promised for those who become Christians.

There is a sixth step in being a Christian. Once you accept Jesus as your Savior, then you're committed to follow Him the rest of your life. The sixth step is "being a Christian." Next week we'll talk about what God has in store for Christians, and what He expects from us.

LESSON FOUR:
IS THIS THE END OF THE ROAD OR JUST THE BEGINNING?

MATERIALS NEEDED FOR LESSON #4:

Opening Activity: Review questions and bag of candy bars

Teaching time:

- Option #2: Bring a bunch of Legos® or some other form of building blocks—enough for each student to have 18-20 identical sets of blocks plus 4 extra sets for you to work with.
- A student workbook for each child for the "Gifts from God" and "What's in Heaven/Not in Heaven" Word Search activities

OBJECTIVES FOR LESSON #4

Our students will come to recognize some of the presents that God gives to Christians. They will also understand that becoming a Christian is just the beginning of a lifelong commitment. They will begin to see what God expects from His children.

OPENING ACTIVITY: (7-10 MINUTES)

Preparation: Come to class with 15-20 review questions covering the last three weeks' lessons. Also come with a bag of small candy bars (enough candy bars for one per question).

*See question page at the back of this lesson for a list of possible review questions. If you need more, don't like these, or they don't fit the activities that you actually did in class, make up your own.

Activity: Ask the class your review questions. As the kids give the correct answers, reward them with a candy bar. Try to give everyone in the class a chance to "win" a candy bar, before you allow a child to answer a second time.

LESSON

PART ONE: WHAT GOD HAS IN STORE FOR CHRISTIANS (10 MINUTES)

Last week we looked at the price that Jesus paid on the cross for our sins.

Do you think that Jesus' dying on the cross could take away every sin in the world? Of course it could.

Has His sacrifice on the cross taken away everyone's sin? No.

Why not? Not everyone has decided to be a Christian.

If His Son has already paid the price, why does God require us to become Christians to have our sins removed? He wants us to choose to love and to follow Him.

Do you remember the second week when we talked about why the tree was in the Garden? Do you remember that God put it there so that Adam and Eve could freely choose to obey him? Remember how the tape recorder had no choice but to say great things about me?

Well, today is just like in the Garden. God has provided one way to enter into His family again (just as Adam and Eve had one way to sin). He has done this so that we can choose to follow Him and to love Him. That is the kind of person that God wants in His family.

Jesus' sacrifice on the cross can take away the sin of every person in the world, but they have to choose to accept the gift from God.

CHRISTMAS MORNING ILLUSTRATION

Think about Christmas for a minute. **What time do you wake up on Christmas morning? Do your parents make you wait until a certain time to open your presents? What do you do when it's finally time to open the gifts?**

Now, what would happen if you woke up Christmas morning, went into the room where the presents were, and saw your name on several of them, but never opened them? Would they still be your gifts? Would you ever get to enjoy them? What if the present you were dying to have this year was in the box, but you never opened it? Would you get to play with it? This is what happens to those who don't accept Christ as their Savior. God has some great gifts in store for them, but they never choose to accept them, so they never receive the benefits of those gifts.

WORKBOOK ACTIVITY Turn to the "God's Gifts to You" page in your student workbook and discover some of the things that God has in store for his children.

WORKBOOK ACTIVITY After completing the gifts page, let the class do the "What's in Heaven/Not in Heaven" Word Search, to remind them of the greatest gift that God has in store for his children.

PART TWO: WHAT DOES GOD EXPECT OF CHRISTIANS?

(Time will depend on which activity you choose.)

When you become a Christian and are baptized, are you done with what God wants you to do? Of course not; it's only the beginning.

What kinds of things do you think God wants Christians to do? Let your class list a variety of answers. Help them think of others if they run out too soon. Some possible answers are: We are to grow up in Christ (become more like him); we are to encourage each other; we are to pray to God; we are to go to church; we are to help those who are in need (food, clothing, friendship); we are to try to obey God to the best of our ability. These things are just a start. As you learn more about Christ, you'll learn how to serve and follow him better.

WHAT DO THESE VERSES TELL US GOD WANTS US TO DO?

Romans 8:13 — Don't live by the sinful nature, but through the Spirit.

Psalm 119:11 — Hide God's word in our hearts.

Psalm 119:17 — Obey the word of God.

Matthew 6:9 — Pray.

Hebrews 13:15 — Praise God.

Hebrews 10:25 — Gather together, go to church.

Philippians 4:8-9 — Think about true, noble, praiseworthy things.

James 1:27 — Take care of the widows and orphans, not being polluted by this world.

This is, of course, just the tip of the iceberg as to what God has to say about what He wants His children to do.

There is one other important thing that we need to start doing immediately, and that is telling others about Christ.

ACTIVITY OPTION #1: THE CHAIN GAME (8-10 MINUTES)

Preparation: none

Activity: Have the class form a circle. You're going to do several short activities going around the circle. Each person is to look to the person on their right side for directions and "pass" on those directions to the person on their left, until they have gone all the way around the circle and returned to the teacher.

Things to pass around the circle:

1. a smile
2. a frown
3. crossed eyes
4. crying
5. jumping for joy
6. any other facial or body expression that you can think of

Now play the telephone game (or gossip game). Whisper a short sentence into the ear of the person on your right. They must whisper it to the person next to them, and so on until it goes all the way around the circle. When it gets back to you, tell the group what you heard. Is it what it started out to be? Remember, each person may only whisper the phrase once. If the person didn't hear it, they have to do the best that they can.

Go around the room 3-4 times with different phrases. It's often funnier if you start out with phrases that say harmless things about people in the room.

Ask the class: **What do these activities teach us about our responsibility to share the Good News of Christ to others?** Direct the answers toward comments along the lines of "We can tell others about Christ with our actions too" and "If they learn about Jesus from us, we had better make sure that we tell them the right things."

ACTIVITY OPTION #2:
BEING BLOCKHEADS FOR CHRIST (20-25 MINUTES)

Preparation: You will need to raid your children's stock of building blocks (Lego or similar) or borrow them from a friend. To get enough blocks you may have to buy your child an extra set or borrow from more than one friend.

Each student needs to have a set of approximately 18 blocks. In addition, you will need four extra sets for yourself. **Each set needs to be identical with regard to shapes but not colors.** In other words, each set needs to be capable of making exactly identical objects. For example each set might contain four 1 x 1 blocks, four 1 x 2 blocks, three 1 x 4 blocks, three 2 x 2 blocks, and four 4 x 2 blocks. You will need to sort them ahead of time so that each child has what they need.

Teachers need to create different objects from each of the four bags of Legos ahead of time. Keep these out of sight of the students.

Activity: You will have a student look at one of the objects and then that student will try to describe the object to the other students in such a way that they will be able to build an identical shape (don't worry about color) with their bag of blocks. This process will be repeated 4 times with specific variations.

1. The first student may look at the prebuilt object only once. After looking at the object, the student may use any means to

communicate the object's shape to the other students. He may talk, demonstrate, point, gesture, whatever, but he may not look at the object again. When the students are satisfied, let them compare their structures to the original.

2. This time the lead student may look as often as she wants at the object (make sure the object is hidden from the view of the rest of the class), but she may not talk or touch any of the blocks. She may only gesture and point. When the students are satisfied, let them compare their structures to the original.

3. This time the lead student may look as often as she wants but may not gesture or point in any way. With her hands behind her back, she must describe the object in such a way that the other students build a similar structure. When the students are satisfied, let them compare their structures to the original.

4. This time the lead student may look as often as she wants, she may use any and all means of communicating how to build the object, including picking up her blocks and modeling how the structure is to be built. When the students are satisfied, let them compare their structures to the original.

Use the following questions to lead a short discussion.

Which method was the hardest? Why? Which method was the easiest? Why?

What was difficult about #1? What was difficult about #2? What was difficult about #3? Why was #4 the easiest?

Apply this to our lives with Christ.

If we hardly ever look at Him, what kind of model are we?

If we talk about Him, but our actions don't show it, what kind of model are we?

If we point out "godly actions," but we don't explain them to others or show them in our lives, how can they come to know Him?

If we model Christ with our actions, how much easier is it for others to come to know him?

If we look to Christ, talk about Him, point out godly actions, and show what it means to be a Christian with our own actions, how much easier would it be for others to come to know Jesus through us?

PART THREE: DOES GOD EXPECT ME TO BE PERFECT?

As we look at the things God wants us to do, it's easy to get intimidated and think that we can't possibly please Him all of the time. So at this point, it's important for us to consider one more aspect of being a member of God's family.

When you become a Christian, does God expect you to be perfect? No, he does not. He knows that you're going to make mistakes.

PARENT WITH BABY ILLUSTRATION

How many of you have younger sisters or brothers? How many of you have been around babies who were just learning to walk? Think about what you saw as their moms and dads were helping them learn to walk. They'd help them up and let the babies hold on to their hands, and then they'd let go and encourage the young children to take a step or two. **What would always happen after they had taken a couple of steps?** That's right, they'd fall down. **Now what would the parents do after the babies fell down?** That's right; they pick them up and give them big hugs, a lot of encouragement, and then they help them to try again. **Have you ever seen a mom or dad watch their little child fall down and then get mad at the baby and yell at it saying, "You should have learned to walk by now?"** Of course not, no loving parent would do that to a little child learning to walk.

That's the way our Father in heaven treats us. He wants us to stop sinning and being disobedient, but He also knows that we will make mistakes and fall down occasionally. When we do, He will pick us up, forgive us, and encourage us to do better next time. He knows that we won't be perfect, but He does expect us to keep trying to do better.

God has promised that as long as we continue to keep Jesus as Lord of our lives and try to obey Him to the best of our ability, He will call us His children and He will continue to forgive us and to love us. He will do this all of our lives until He welcomes us into heaven to be with Him forever.

CLOSING: (5 MINUTES)

We've spent the past four weeks teaching you about what it means to be a Christian, what God has done for us, and what we need to do in order to receive the promised gifts that God has in store for us.

Now, we're going to give you a chance to respond. But you need to know a couple of things first.

- You don't have to become a Christian just because you've gone to this class. If you're not ready yet to make that decision, you can wait.
- You don't have to go through this class to become a Christian. This class is just here to help answer your questions.
- The decision that you make today would simply be that you want one of the ministers to come visit you and your parents to talk about this decision. Your parents will play a part in this decision because God has called them to raise you to the best of their ability. They may tell you to wait a little while longer, or they may say yes. That's between you, them, and God. If you think you're ready to make this decision, you need to tell your parents about it.

DECISION CARD

Preparation: Make enough copies of the decision cards (next page), so that each of your children can fill one out.

Hand out the cards and have your kids fill them out. Tell them to check the line of the three choices which fits them. Even if they've already decided for Christ, have them fill out the card. After everyone is finished, have them turn the cards back in to you.

If any of your kids indicate that they're ready, contact their parents with this information and give the card to your minister.

SOME POSSIBLE REVIEW QUESTIONS:

1. **What is a Christian?** "Someone who believes and follows the teachings of Christ," "They are Christlike," or "One who has accepted Jesus as the Lord of their Life and Savior."

2. **What is our basic definition for sin?** Sin is being disobedient to God.

NAME _____

____ I am already a Christian

____ I want to think about it some more

____ I would like to be baptized and have one of the ministers
      come visit me and my parents in my home

Parent's name _____

Address _____

Phone _____ Email _____

- -

NAME _____

____ I am already a Christian

____ I want to think about it some more

____ I would like to be baptized and have one of the ministers
      come visit me and my parents in my home

Parent's name _____

Address _____

Phone _____ Email _____

3. **Name three other names or titles for Jesus?** See "Names of Jesus" worksheet.

4. **Who has sinned?** Everyone, except Jesus.

5. **What did the paper fort game and "The Monkey Trap" teach us about sin?** "It confines us," "It traps us," "It seems fun at first," etc.

6. **What was the first sin?** Adam and Eve eating of the fruit of the tree of the knowledge of good and evil.

7. **What punishment did Adam and Eve face?** Eve would have pain in childbirth; Adam would have to work the land for food. They were kicked out of the Garden; they would grow old and die. They would face a judgment day.

8. **What is Hell going to be like?** See "What Is Hell Like?" worksheet.

9. **Why did God put the tree in the Garden?** So that Adam and Eve would have a choice to stay in the Garden with Him.

10. **What did the Old Testament laws teach us?** What sin is and that we can't do it alone. We need a Savior.

11. **What did the sacrificing of animals teach us?** That the punishment for sin is death, and that only something (someone) that is pure can cleanse us.

12. **What did the Civil War draft illustrate to us about God's plan?**

Someone who wasn't "drafted" could take our place for us.

13. **What does archery have to do with teaching us about God's plan?** It was another description for sin: missing the target that God has set for us.

14. **What price did Jesus pay for our sins?** The pain of the trial, and dying on the cross

15. **What two parts of the plan of salvation did the spaghetti and marshmallow teach us?** Hearing and believing

16. **What are the other three steps in God's plan?** Repent, confess, be baptized.

17. **What did the flash paper (or cross and sin sheets) teach us?** God will wipe our sins away through the blood of Jesus.

18. **What is the sixth step in the five steps of God's plan?** Living the Christian life, which is our topic for today.

ANSWERS TO WORKBOOK ACTIVITIES

WHAT DOES IT MEAN?

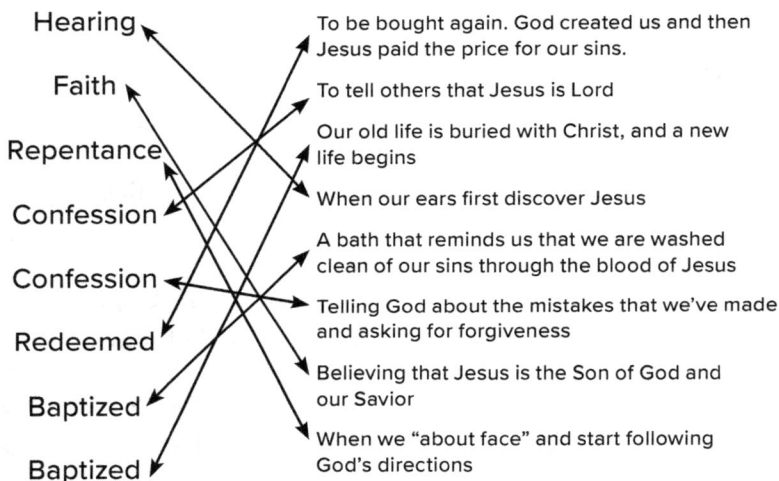

Hearing — To be bought again. God created us and then Jesus paid the price for our sins.

Faith — To tell others that Jesus is Lord

Repentance — Our old life is buried with Christ, and a new life begins

Confession — When our ears first discover Jesus

Confession — A bath that reminds us that we are washed clean of our sins through the blood of Jesus

Redeemed — Telling God about the mistakes that we've made and asking for forgiveness

Baptized — Believing that Jesus is the Son of God and our Savior

Baptized — When we "about face" and start following God's directions

GOD'S GIFTS TO YOU FILL-IN-BLANK LIST

For God so **L O V E D** the world

Our Savior: **J E S U S**

God's messengers: **A N G E L S**

Lots of food: **F E A S T**

God's chair: **T H R O N E**

Jesus' Father: **G O D**

Followers of Christ: **C H R I S T I A N S**

Streets of **G O L D**

Choir singing **S O N G S**

Opposite of: Darkness is **L I G H T**

Old is **N E W**

Sadness is **J O Y**

THINGS IN HEAVEN

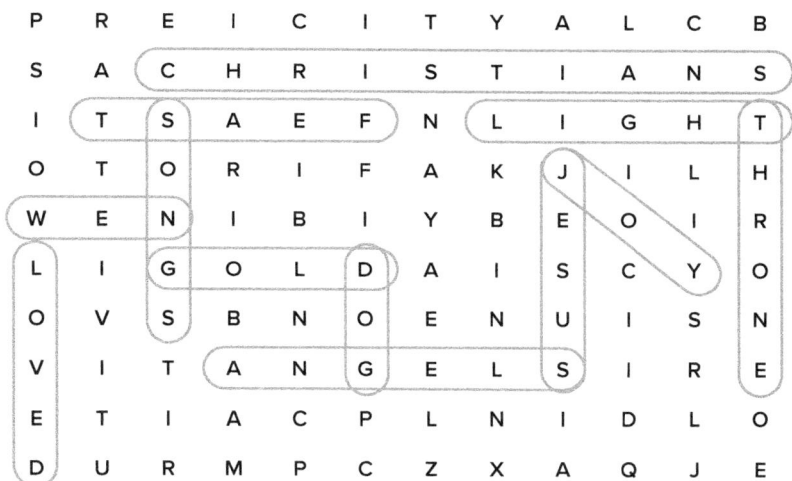

P	R	E	I	C	I	T	Y	A	L	C	B
S	A	C	H	R	I	S	T	I	A	N	S
I	T	S	A	E	F	N	L	I	G	H	T
O	T	O	R	I	F	A	K	J	I	L	H
W	E	N	I	B	I	Y	B	E	O	I	R
L	I	G	O	L	D	A	I	S	C	Y	O
O	V	S	B	N	O	E	N	U	I	S	N
V	I	T	A	N	G	E	L	S	I	R	E
E	T	I	A	C	P	L	N	I	D	L	O
D	U	R	M	P	C	Z	X	A	Q	J	E

THINGS NOT IN HEAVEN

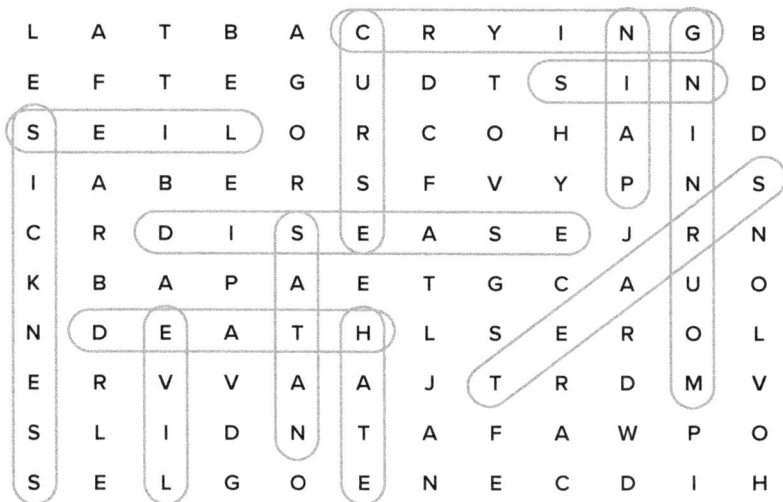

L	A	T	B	A	C	R	Y	I	N	G	B
E	F	T	E	G	U	D	T	S	I	N	D
S	E	I	L	O	R	C	O	H	A	I	D
I	A	B	E	R	S	F	V	Y	P	N	S
C	R	D	I	S	E	A	S	E	J	R	N
K	B	A	P	A	E	T	G	C	A	U	O
N	D	E	A	T	H	L	S	E	R	O	L
E	R	V	V	A	A	J	T	R	D	M	V
S	L	I	D	N	T	A	F	A	W	P	O
S	E	L	G	O	E	N	E	C	D	I	H

NOTES

www.ingramcontent.com/pod-product-compliance
Lightning Source LLC
Chambersburg PA
CBHW060041050426

42448CB00012B/3095